# UNBRIDLED

An anthology of women's poems

edited by Magi Gibson

This paperback was first published in 2023 by

## WomanWord

Glasgow

Introduction © Magi Gibson

Brirish Library Cataloguing-in-Publication Data
A catalogue for this book is available on request from the British Library.
ISBN 9780956905628

Typesetting & Cover Design by WomanWord
©WomanWord

# The Scold's Bridle

Scold's bridles, also known as witch's bridles, branks or jougs were in use between 1550 and 1800 as punishment devices for women who were judged to talk too much, to express views unacceptable to the society and culture of the time, and who could not be silenced by other means.

Made of leather and iron or a mix of both, they were locked onto a woman's head to silence and shame her.

The scold's bridle was part of a wider culture of fear and punishment of witches and other unconventional women whose views and voices were deemed dangerous.

The first written reference to a Scold's Bridle is in 1653 in the Lanark Borough Records in Scotland.

As well as punishing and silencing the individual woman, its use was intended as a harsh lesson to other women to be cautious in their speech.

for all the warrior women

# Contents

# INTRODUCTION by Magi Gibson

In 2023, I was invited to the Forth Valley Feminist Conference in Scotland
to deliver a talk on Women's Poetry of Witness, Protest and Dissent. In
the talk I referenced poets who'd deeply affected and inspired me by their
ability to blend the political with the poetic. Poets like Adrienne Rich, Maya
Angelou, Audre Lorde, the amazingly brave Indian Tamil poet, Salma and
the Polish poet, Anna Swir.

I also explained that I was about to start work on an anthology
of contemporary women's poetry - an anthology I hoped would reflect
the qualities of Witness, Protest, Dissent. I asked women to send me their
poems, even if they hadn't written poetry before. I stressed both the potency
and the importance of poetry, quoting Audre Lorde who said in her 1977
essay, *Poetry is not a Luxury*, "Poetry is not only dream and vision; it is the
skeleton architecture of our lives."

Women have been punished for millennia for being outspoken, for
not toeing the line. For being brave enough to break from the herd, brave
enough to speak up against restrictions imposed on them, to ask for rights
denied them. For this, they were name-called, beaten, shamed, vilified,
raped, stoned, drowned, burned at the stake. Historically, the 'chilling factor'
on women's freedom of speech and artistic expression has been very icy
indeed.

The ages of the women featured here range from a 14 year old still
at school, to a mature woman in her 70s. These are women who live in
Scotland, Ireland, England, Wales, Spain, America and Australia. They
come from a mix of heritages and social backgrounds. They rage at the
world's injustices and use that rage to fuel explosive, gut-wrenching, glori-
ously defiant poetry. They use their love for humanity to create poetry of
celebration of womanhood, of tenderness, of love.

Dip into this book and you will find myriad aspects of being a
woman today explored through multiple poetic approaches. Greek and

Celtic myth feature, as well as references to historic and recent events.

Discover here poetry that reflects on defining moments in a woman's life, from first menstrual bleeding to first sexual awakening, from the tragically all-too-common experience of molestation, to miscarriages, births, infertility, hysterectomies and the growing acceptance of the female body as it ages.

There are poems within these pages that explore sex and sexuality, interrogate feminism, celebrate the sense of empowerment that comes from finding common cause with other women. With passion and defiance these poets bear witness, they question, they protest, they dissent. In short, they do the important and culturally vital job of creating *the skeleton architecture of their lives* in the twenty-first century.

The Polish poet, Anna Swir, wrote, "The poet has a conscience with room to grow. What does not, as yet, shock and outrage others, shocks and outrages her."

I would like to thank the poets in this anthology for providing a bold and living example of the truth of Anna Swir's statement.

It is alarming, however, that due to the recent outbreak of censoriousness in the arts a number of these poets feel they cannot be published under their real names for fear of damage to careers, artistic 'cancellation', or simply to protect their children and families.

What an indictment of the current cultural climate that we have regressed to an age where so many women feel safer using a pseudonym or Anon. Scold's Bridles may now be in glass cases in our museums, but this new twenty-first century version of attempting to silence women who dare to be free-thinkers is every bit as nasty.

Finally, a huge thank you to all the poets featured here, and to all who helped and supported me in bringing this poetry anthology to fruition. An anthology that above all sings defiantly of the living, breathing, everyday reality of womanhood.

*Magi Gibson, October 2023*

# I am

Do not question my femininity
I am the female, I am the feminine
It flows within me like the river to the sea
It flows within me like the power of ice down a valley
It flows like lava creating new worlds, new life
from the power of me

Do not twist my feminine to mean shaved & preened
& squeezed & tucked, pushed up & plucked
& dyed & make-upped

My pain is not meant to please you
My pain does not set me free
It binds me like the corset & heels
the symbols given to me to be
who I am
but that is not who I am
that is your version, your corruption
of my feminine

I am life    I am blood    I am rage

I am a million screams of a million women beaten
into silence by your restrictions & rules
I am rape    FGM    infanticide
I am the witch you burnt at the stake

I am a witch you drowned in the lake
I am the one you bought and sold for pleasure
I am the mother the daughter the sister
the aunt the grandmother and wife
I am the alpha and omega of life

You call me weak yet I am the power of creation
the bedrock of family and civilisation
I have raised the world in my womb
You have life because I gave it to you

I am foot-binding, I am menstruation huts
I am a prisoner in my own home
I am rage

I am honour killings, child brides and forced marriage
I am the rage of a million dreams un-lived
I am the denial of an education
I am the denial of my abilities
I am the one stoned to death when it was you
who violated me

I am rage

I am *what was she wearing?*
I am *how much did she drink?*
I am *she was asking for it*
I am trafficked
I am a sex industry slave
I am not empowered by it

I am rage

I am shamed for using my breasts to feed my baby
I am praised for using my breasts for Page 3
I am the one who had to die for my rights
I am the one who still doesn't have those rights
I am mocked because I bleed
I am the body parts
I am the breast, the lips, legs and arse
used to sell you aftershave or fast cars

I am rage

I am pain overlooked and symptoms ignored
I am the goddess your Holy Book forgot to include
I am the history not taught
I am a scarlet letter, I am the fallen women
I am the Magdalene laundry captive

I am rage

I am domestic violence, I am revenge porn
I am stalked, I am the other end
of your wolf whistle
I am told it's a compliment
I am told to smile

I am rage

I am a link in the chain of suffering and pain

that stretches back to my birthing of this world

I am the meaning of the word survivor
I am the power, I am the warrior
I am the protector and provider

I am an unstoppable force
I am the force you underestimated
I am the force you can never understand

I am She

And that's why you corrupt what is mine
the sacred feminine and holy divine

You fear the day I rise up
You fear the day I say enough is enough
You fear that I will do to you
what has been done to us

I am rage


*Aja The Empress*

# The Sky is a Woman

What else
swells and bellows,
then empties to give life;
tussles with the sea
but lets him think he broke the ships;
hears her strength christened fury
yet emits her unending warmth.
She will souse the city unpredictably.
She has ways to burn it too.
Her aging, timeless face contains the glitter
of Andromeda, streaked with shimmering scars.
Most nights she lets others shine, does not
keep track. Stands ready to disarm the dark
pink cut of new conviction
or the honeyed threat of gloom.
Provident, multifaceted sibyl;
it is not your pull that holds her here.

*Marisa Campbell*

# Cíoch

*I gcuimhne Ann Lovett, 1984*


An raibh deacracht ag An Leanbh Íosa
Greim ceart a fháil ar chíoch a mháthar,
Ar chaoin siad beirt le frustrachas?
Ar tháinig maistíteas uirthise
Leis an strus ar fad – torrach gan choinne,
Gan trácht ar an ghráin i súile
Iósaef ar an bhóthar go Beithil – agus
An chúlchaint ó na comharsana?

Ar an altóir, tá fear
Nár shil bainne cíche riamh síos a éide aifrinn,
Nár luigh i bhfolcadh sáile riamh lena shiní nimhneacha a chneasú,
Nár gearradh a ghabhal riamh leis an bhreith a éascú,
Nár tugadh sopastóir dó, ná peasaire, ná ola ricne féin.

Gan fuil.
Gan allas.
Gan deora.
Seasann sé ansin, ag léamh ón Leabhar
Fá bhreith an Linbh, Íosa.

Ní ar Ann, máthair Mhuire, atá mo smaointe
I mo shuí ag cúl an tséipéil,
Ach ar an Ann eile

A fuair bás uaigneach, eaglach.
Cloíte.
Gan tearmann, gan dídean,
Ag cosa na maighdine
I Longfort

*Réaltán Ní Leannáin*

# Breast

*In memoriam Ann Lovett, RIP 1984*

Did the Baby Jesus have difficulty
Latching on to his mother's breast,
Did they both cry with frustration?
Did she get mastitis
With all the stress – unexpectedly pregnant, and the contempt
In Joseph's eyes on the way to Bethlehem,
And the neighbours' gossip?

On the altar, a man
Who never ever leaked milk down his Mass garments,
Who never lay in a salt bath to heal his sore nipples,
Whose crotch was never torn to ease the birth,
Never had a suppository, nor pessary, nor even castor oil.

Bloodless.
Sweat-free.
No tears.
He stands there, reading from the book
Of the birth of the Child Jesus.

I don't think of Ann, Mary's mother,
from my seat at the back of the chapel,

But of the other Ann
Who died a lonely, fearful death,
Destroyed.
No shelter, no sanctuary,
At the feet of the Virgin
In Longford

*Réaltán Ní Leannáin*

# Salt In The Mouth

There are many ways to kill a woman.
For baby girls a handful of salt in the mouth,
A dry drowning, the silencing crystals,
A deadly sea surge, the corrosive breath,
Then silence and blank-eyed denial.

There are many ways to kill a woman.
The methodical unstitching of our minds
Picked away in scatters of bloody threads
Snipped out and obliterated in anguish and despair,
Then silence and blank-eyed denial.

There are many ways to kill a woman.
The knife, the gun, the fists, the broken hyoid,
Our killers are inventive creatures yet banal,
Like all evil they exist in endless repetition
And then in silence and blank-eyed denial.

*Joolz Denby*

# The Table

A woman full of the contentment of living comes home, and puts her phone on the table. Lights her favourite candle and puts it down there, she puts the tea and the chocolate on the table. She puts the grey, overcast sky and spattering rain on the table. The steamy, damp bus with the broken bits of chatter she puts on the table too. Next to them she puts the cheerful jangling sounds of the coins in the till and the 'thank you' from the woman at the shop. She carefully placed her Roisin, snuggling and sleepy on the table. Beside her, on the table she placed the memory of her girls excited and sparkly eyed watching Goosebumps on Sunday afternoon. Her hopes and fears for her future she laid down on the table. The people she loved were placed on the table and a few she despised were put there too. Her longing to be more was placed on the table alongside the certainty she was going in the right direction. The table was large and strong for an IKEA coffee table, and it stood solid under the weight she piled upon it. She smiled to herself, thanked it, and not for the first time considered it £35 well spent.

*Sharon Frame*

# It Wasn't A Woman

who used a stick to abort the baby in an 11 year old girl
who gang-raped a 4 year old who took a girl
to a room of shamrock green rugby shirts, later texting
about spit roast and sluts who gave money
to a rag-picker and took one of her five
to a faraway brown-dust city who sold her on to the businessmen
it wasn't a woman who beat the children with an iron bar
so that vertebrae were crushed it wasn't a woman
who ruptured the rectum of a small boy who broke the vagina
of a baby girl it wasn't a woman who scalded a wife
because she spoke to another man who flung acid
in the face of a girl who did not want to marry
who poured acid on a wife's genitals
it wasn't a woman who broke a nose blackened an eye
bit a cheek so that the marks of those teeth
are a tell-tale circle of pits in the skin
it wasn't a woman whose breasts were purple and green
whose pregnant belly was a violet bruise
whose child was punched out of her so she bled to death
it wasn't a woman who rejected those twin girls
it wasn't a woman who burned a widow to death
who shouted at a wife in the rich people's shopping mall
who forced her to have sex who took the children away
who kept all the money who called out names like dog
and here, bitch, who put a collar around her neck
then led her on all fours around the apartment

who smashed her favourite things
who kept a gun beside the bed and threatened to use it
who blamed her even as he punched her
roared the rhythms of cunt-face cunt-face cunt-face
because it helped him hit harder it wasn't a woman
whose lips were scissored to shreds by those knuckles
it wasn't a woman it wasn't a woman it wasn't a woman

*Mary O'Donnelll*

# RAGE

I don't know why I keep listening to the news I don't know why
my neighbours want to destroy the lush green lindens where
baby birds are nesting I don't know why I never turned into a
decent housewife but I'm not though I'm proud of my shelves
stacked with books I don't know why I'm allergic to house dust
when my home is knee-deep in the stuff & allergic to pollen
when I love trees I suspect god's a bastard & thinks it's a joke
I don't know why they push refugees back into the Medi-
terranean at midnight & think we won't care why they lock
migrant children up in the desert in Texas lonely & scared
& call it Camp Bliss why they pollute the air & pretend it's
okay while the ice sheets melt & whole species die – I mean
WTF? – I don't know why we have such wretched pover-
ty in a world that's so rich why they experiment on kids with
surgery and drugs & call it kindness & say it's care why they
lock male thugs in prison with women & claim that it's fair

but I do know this:

I love the smell of washing fresh off the line I love how each year
ragged skeins of geese appear honking loudly in the
winter sky how human hair is strong as steel how
an octopus has three hearts and blood that's blue
& I love how my heart races when I'm close to you
I don't know why I find it hard to write these days
but I guess I'm scared of so much rage at those with the power

fucking us over & I do know enough about long dormant
volcanoes that it's best seriously it's best
that they don't
erupt


Magi Gibson

# Erasure

what is it about (me)
you are so afraid of?

every time I dare / think
I am drawn in permanent marker

you take something      away

and I realise to you I am
only an idea sketched in soft 2B
/vulnerable to your fingertips

I rub my eyes (gently) and try
to understand your endgame:

do you want      me to not be?
do you want      to be me?

you smell victory either way
but really, have you thought this through?

as you sharpen your pencil
to imagine me again
getting smaller all the time
(but point well made)

you will only have yourself to blame

*Liz Houchin*

# Women

I sail into the world of women,
in a magnificent ship that does not interest them.

I imagine this is what loving them is:
adding up the piecework of them,

the pale neck, the sudden crow's feet,
The expensive lips saying of course of course.

I have learned their language, I can say
What do you think? like a native,

but they detect an accent in spite of me.
Their eyes rest on me over the wine.

Their secrets are palpable as money.
We trade, and I grow rich. I feel free.

We compare songs, the cuts on our wrists.
Sometimes I think I have found my home.

When I hold them, I hear their bones crying.
Their costly hair drifts and shines.

*Polly Clark*

# Talking to My Husband in the Wardrobe

It's not mice or rats nor a cat in the yard
not the sound of intruders downstairs.

I know you are in there, telescoped shut
breathing in the ghost of my perfume.

I see you burying your nose in the hot pink folds —
my ball gown — shot silk and taffeta.

I wonder why the flesh of your muscular thigh
is enamoured of my pearl-studded dress.

What is the etiquette in cases such as this?
The question is nothing if not delicate.

Though I hear you most nights
scuffling in my closet

I've now stopped wondering
how you get in.

*Abigail Ottley*

# Which of Us Was Blinded

There might have been a snake but there was no
handy stick. No blind prophet of Apollo like Tiresias.
That was another tale entirely. No drunken god
with a bone to pick spoiling for an after-party fight.

Your trick, your metamorphosis, was simpler,
more brutal. The blow you delivered sent me reeling.
Afterward, you cried as if you were the victim.
Insisted I surely must have known.

How could I have guessed what you kept so close
lulling me with your lattice-work of lies?
All the lesser betrayals I fancied I might find
fell short of the truth by country miles.

Turning the key I had stolen from your dresser
I came like a thief into your kingdom. Behold!

Your costumes hanging in racks and rows
your wig stands and your size ten stilettos.

There were photographs.
A brilliant sea.
For a time I believed I might drown.

Which of us was blinded? I think of it like this.

I brought my night scope.
Finding you in my sights at last
my inner eye opened
in a flash.

*Abigail Ottley*

# She Remembers Her Husband As Proteus

You slipped through my fingers
like water, morphed

into whatever you wanted to be:
a tree, a wild pig,

a howling wind. You knew
all the angles, the smart street moves,

you had aliases. It was no big deal,
merely paper and ink

and you lied for fun, so I still don't know
if your father was an embezzler:

even your dog
had a bank account with Lloyds

*Abigail Ottley*

# Bodysnatcher

Your branches a backlit
brawl. Spiky fingers
stuck up at the snobby moon.

I feel your sly call,
broach your heavy
shadow's undertow.

A crackle in my bones;
now I'm the jagged tangle,
the grim knots, sour nodes
of discontent, self-pity.
I am the dark tree

while you dawdle on,
cadging a new ballgown off the sky,
willing yourself into a skin of flowers.

*Katherine Duffy*

# Gynarchy in the UK

Hi my name is Karen
your oedipal overlord
surrogate bosom
Seek safety and comfort
in the darkness
of my cave, my
G-Y-N ANARCHY

You will respect the erect
spectre of my protection shelter

Don't ever move your head,
never see your shadow, what's real
is what I tell you

I'm your smothering mothering
killer of life, I fight your battles
so you don't have to

Woman is the trigger
of the world
I know how to hold you
you're my gun
my beautiful son
my work here is done

So let's baptise you in the fire
of combat you coward

Hang your head you pathetic
vile varlet

Eurgh! You're just like your father!
You kill what you can't take care of

Anyway Norman, stick the kettle on
and I'll lift up my skirt -
crawl back up where you came from


*Louise Distras*

# Clogher Road Gothic

bent over, a wizened sceach man slams
his shovel sharply into the ground
behind his low pebble dash
Sunday gardening the pleasures

& flings a grey wet
something up and onto the silvery
blade wire rolls that crown
the walls of the substation next door

where it hangs
dripping dark red
its rodent tail twitching

even the crows are repulsed

I look from five-metre-high hanging blood rat
to man & back & he gives me a stare
that says you could be next
swinging up there        jog on

*Estelle Birdy*

# Inherited Defiance

On the bus to Falkirk
I cradle Granny in the palm of my hand.
An unadorned urn – not her taste at all
she liked colour, and candour
a headscarf fluttering in buttercup yellow
a handbag rattling with lipsticks – buttery stumps
in Revlon Red.

My own colours are muted
as a man sits opposite me, leans forward.
I hug the urn close to my chest.

*SMILE*, he says to me
in the imperative case
in the language of command
*SMILE*.

My smile is a switchblade
passed down like the knowledge of blood
through generations of women.

Are you sure you want me to wield it?

Instead I picture him in an ash-cloud
gagging on my granny.
I'm sure she'd approve.

A final act of love,
humour
and inherited defiance.

*Kathryn Robertson*

# Strangers On a Train

You catch my eye.
The look
flashes between us.
A look that's travelled across centuries
etching itself into our DNA.
I recognise it even in a face
I don't know.
The seismic shift
creeps in.
Gooseflesh arms, hair on end,
clenched spines.
In a flicker, we are familiar.
We synchronise.

His breath wafts too close,
his gaze lasts too long,
his flesh spills over the boundary and relaxes like it's taken up residence.

He's unaware of the old pact
signed in the bloodstain of sisterhood;
bonds formed in fields, laundries, factories -
a million journeys.
He's unaware of the silent exchange,
the story we just shared.

'Hello!' I call across the gulf.
'Didn't see you there.'

And I could cry
at the relief
in your eyes.

You grab your bags,
and, for the first time, smile,
hurry across the aisle – 'Hi.'

And he shrinks
back to normal size.

*Dis_critic*

# How To Be A Stalker

He said:       You are a beautifully souled car crash of a woman
I want to save and adore and own.

He said:       You hurt my feelings last night, you little bitch.
Stop playing games with me, you know
we were meant to be together...

He said:       I know you could call the police on me again,
but I'm banking that you're not so cruel...

He said:       You are disgusting.
You man-hating whore.
You will be with cats forever.

He said:       You will die alone.

*Jenny Lindsay*

# my friend's vagina

i won't lie it is difficult not to wonder
what life will be like if you lose your job
and we have to move from this unaffordable
suburb by the sea. i text my friend, though
i should be writing—i gave up one day of salary
to do this. i call her my friend though our relationship
is a mere twelve months old. she has a dog called
gypsy me a dog called hector her husband has
no kidneys. her varicose veins bulged—shone blue
through her tight white pants. she had them removed—the
veins not the pants, i want to say publicly, but what
i mean is on the public system. they went in through
her groin. some days after the op i bumped into her in
the supermarket. she lifted her dress showed me the
scar she was wearing no knickers, sent me a text later
to thank me for letting her show me her vagina in the
super market. she is unperturbable a deep thinker an analyser
too much time on her hands in kidney wards she imagines
where else she might be—some weeks it's the back streets
of prague, others the upper east side, once upon a time,
shanghai. i tell her this constant living in her imagination
is her way of coping with a husband who has no kidneys
and a dyalisis machine in the lounge room that does not
match the stag's head nor the map of africa with the
seychelles circled by her in black biro.

and she does not disagree. she is open to frankness
she is wise, sage-like, the insights of a monk, she shaved
her head once. she is my go to place when my mojo sags,
when my full moon wanes, when the feathers in my internal
doona need fluffing. my text is frantic—but where will
we go if he loses his job and we have to move from this unaffordable
suburb by the sea? she would have been in the kidney
ward when my text arrived, deep in the turquoise ocean
of her imagination,  it doesn't really matter
where you go, she texted, the unhappiness
inside you will find you. and just as i'm thinking
maybe she'd shaved her head again another
text came through, in saying that she added, i've
always rather fancied acapulco.


*Ali Whitelock*

# On Metaphor

I never realised how apt
those old comparisons of female parts

to roses in particular—metaphysical lines
on love, lushness and moisture,

or petals in tactile frills—until the day
I soaped and washed my mother

in her shower-chair,
saw her labia in its dying glory.

Like any late autumn rose,
her petals, hanging loose, had shrivelled,

awaiting the slightest wintry wind
to blow them free.

Even so, I write of them with love,
the metaphysics of a woman's

life in transit, this aged Venus
eclipsed by time.

*Mary O'Donnell*

# Shela-na-gig

Splay-thighed moon-belly sister
you stare defiance
with your four wide eyes
you grin wild mischief
with your two broad smiles
you dare mild-mannered men
and lady-labelled women
to hold your brazen gaze.

How much I long to be like you!
Naked and true, never hiding
your lustful light below
the bush of false modesty.

How many curious eyes have dropped
their lids before your honesty?
How many more have stopped to stare
and wonder what unhallowed hands would dare
to sculpt you from cold stone?

They tried to kill you once,
called you shameless, harlot, whore
burned you with their righteous indignation
drowned you for the open invitation
you give for fun and fornication.

Perhaps they feared your bold reminder –
we are born of women, are not gods.

Shela-na-gig – old lady who squats
La Que Saba, weathered by centuries
of storm and scorn -

when the moon is full
and the stars are birling wildly in the sky
do you leap around our winter fields
running with the old grey wolves
baubo-belly-dancing
so Demeter will laugh again
and raise Persephone
from the underworld's dark tomb?


*Magi Gibson*

# Manko Taboo

We all use whatever tools are to hand.
In the case of Good for Nothing Girl —
Rokudenashiko — it was a body part,
her red lotus flower, her vulva.  The aim was
to reclaim it from myth and magic and own it
like she owns her eyes, nose and ears.
No more amazing, no less. Such was her defence
when accused of being merely vulgar.

She created a cast, gingerly patting
plaster of Paris into every crevice and fold,
leaving it to prove. Satisfied she worked
the image free as if peeling delicate petals
or a sea anemone and set it to print on a 3D printer,
then shaped it into a full-scale skin kayak,
or canoe, lowered herself in and told the Inuit
she was claiming it back from Man-boat
to Woman-boat then set it afloat
to slice through the swollen water
with her double-bladed paddle in a true line.
Navigating by her inner Attitude Indicator no yawing
now off course. Having taken full possession
of the boat shaped in the curve of a smiling mouth,
she declared herself whole and all at sea.

*Jean O'Brien*

# I am not a Dress

We are women, we are warriors of steel.
Woman is something no man will ever feel.
Woman is not a skill that any man can hone.
Woman is our word and it is ours alone.

I am not a dress to be worn on a whim,
A man in a dress is nonetheless a him.
Women are not simply what we wear.
If this offends you, I do not care.

I am not an idea in any man's mind
And my purpose in life is not to be kind.
So while my rights are trampled every day of the week,
I will not stand by being docile and meek.

I am not defined by sexist lies.
There is more to woman than that shallow guise,
That guise of dresses, bikinis and skirts.
Those clothes are not what womanhood is worth.

I am not a bitch, a TERF, a whore, a slag,
Hysterical, a witch, a slut, a hag.
No! I am a woman, I am a female,
Who will not let her rights be put up for sale.

I am not defined by what men are not.
So to hell with cis misogynistic rot.
I am a woman, I'm not a subset of my sex.
If this makes me a dinosaur, so be it, I'm a T-Rex!

I am not a bleeder nor a menstruator,
A womb carrier or uterus haver.
Those words and phrases are such a sham.
Just call me woman, it is who I am.

We are women, we are warriors of steel.
Woman is something no man will ever feel.
Woman is not a skill that any man can hone.
Woman is our word and it is ours alone.


*Brandubh*

# The Heart of the House

Let them call our bodies haunted houses
where the ghosts never actually lived at all.

Let them call us barren
husks     flushed tombs.
Gardens become graveyards, they sing,
in the absence of our spurts
and our sprucings.

You need stronger foundations,
perhaps a fountain, they trill,
suggesting improvements,
those amateur interior designers
with the wrong tools.

This complex, delicate structure
will liquefy and bloat.
Putrefied lungs will not
be sparked back tae life
no matter how good
their electricians.

As they fill our spaces with their ideas
they will tell us to have no fear—
despite the bodies they've left
in our basements, and the boots,
the muddied, bloodied boots everywhere.

Let them
Let them

Let them rebuild us in
their image of perfection:
mibbes a flashy play mansion
or 50s sink-chained pleasant,
backlash angels mounted
in the entrance hall
frilly gingham kitchen
bleached lawn
shaved hillock
plucked splinters

Let them comment on our handles.
Let them rip down the monthly cleansing rota—
call it outdated     surplus to requirements
Let them misunderstand how
this house breathes a sigh of relief
at the order of our ageing facilities
Let them never mind it
Let them take it away
steam out our netherbows.

Let them make us ghosts in our own haunted houses
Let them market us as in need of a re-fit
too old for selling for a premium as is—
who would buy this through desire alone?
A project, that's how you sell this one, brothers
Drape some fairy-lights around the backlash angels
Trim the wings tae genteel

Now promote us in an advertising brochure
with a squeaky clean plasticky mmm overtone,
a picture of the facade from a decade ago.

Let them.
Let them.

Witches  spinsters       batshit madams   harridans
ladies                   bitches          WOMEN

the heart of the house

We will not rest
We will not cease
We are all we are
We are all we ever were
And some will miss us.

*Jenny Lindsay*

# Weighing Heavy

*Església de Sant Joan Baptista*

She was not enough, you see
for the haloed men
freeze framed in a party game
above the altar on a Deian hill

So they put her to the side
and raised her on a plinth
drowned in coffin satin
snow white and baby blue

They grew her hair to her waist
laced in veil to cover her ears
so she could not hear
the women, hear herself

She was not enough, you see,
so they weighed her down
with a crown on her hot scalp
a metal jaw open like a trap

*Liz Houchin*

# Renaissance He/Him

Renaissance individualism
finds its heir
in the pronouns-in-bio male artist.

A true genius,
perfecting in marble
the grandeur of his humility.

Above, the punishing hand
of his conception
points a finger —

not a threat
but a promise,
born out of compassion.

The visual evidence
is never as important
as the story.

A creation myth
that lectures Anonymous
on her privilege.

Her proportions
deformed
compared to anatomical drawings.

A lived experience
that he can't find
anywhere in the literature.

In this epic of identity,
mastery,
and the consequences of expression,

reputation
is a bloody battleground
with only one canon.

A side of history
neither virgin nor whore
have ever entered.

But he is cut from
a different cloth,
and waves the flag when required.

And claims not to notice
when the institutions he routinely decries
work in tandem at his behest.

The initiated
have faith in his vision,
and so excuse his methods,
citing his exceptionalism among men.

The intensity of emotion,
the scale and volume of the work,
are only proof of his greatness.

After all,
not much was heard from Shakespeare's sister
after the Open Letter.

*Nicole Jones*

# The teacher's lovely long red nails

The teacher's hair was a dark
delicate hill where the wind would stir
a story: three hundred years, three hundred...

My mother at the Belfast sink
in the cold scullery washed clothes, watched
us out of the smallest window.

The teacher said to use all our
crayons. I lathered Fionnuala in pink
and orange, made her stretch a wing over

her brothers to keep them warm.
Lir's lonely daughter, we sang
in choir. The night stars. The wind across

Lough Derravaragh. I leaned on dark
blue. The Sea of Moyle. The teacher's
lovely long red nails. Easy, my mother said,

turning off the single brass tap,
when you've no scrubbing to do. Aoife,
doled as comfort to a widowed king,

changed the Children, sent them out
to live on three different kinds of water.
I made waves like the edge of a saw,

flew notes from the swans' yellow beaks,
because afterwards she felt a bit sorry
and allowed them still to speak and sing.

A small, cloaked figure by a lake.
I took care with her eyes — fine black
lines to let her see what she had made.

*Katherine Duffy*

'and the angel of the lord appeared to him,
and said to him, "the lord is with you,
O mighty man of valour"
[judges 6:12]'

her eyes are *blootered / swollen like the
plums that were not in the ice box / but knee-deep
by the river rotting in torrential scottish
rain / they were bruised & slimy / burst & oozing /
he was probably saving them for breakfast /

Question
    what do you tell a woman with two black eyes?

Answer
    nothing, you already told her twice**

the photo of my parents on their wedding
day is torn in half / held together by the twenty
four hour emergency plumbing magnet stuck to
the door of my westinghouse where i hang all
memories requiring refrigeration / in my

father's half he looks like a boy in a hired
evening suit / his brylcreemed hair peaking to
attention like the great wave off kanagawa / his
legs are spread hands clasped ring finger sporting
the knuckle duster he would cherish from that day

forward for richer, for poorer, in sickness &
increasing sickness /

in her torn half she stands meek / stiff
as the plastic bride on top of their
3 tier weding cake / her stilettos sunk so deep
into the icing they have reached the marzipan /

in the years that followed she would obey &
forsake / take the hammer & smash the ring
with which she he wed / walk into endless
doors / set fire to her white lace dress / swallow
the tut tuts from the good women in line at the
bakery / each teetering precariously on the fragile
shells of their own hypocritical meringues
whispering, look at the bruises would you …
why in god's name does she stay?

*Ali Whitelock*

* *blooter, blouter, bluiter n. and v. [ blʌutər, blutər] — to obliterate, strike
excessively hard [often refers to a football]*

** *In 2023, this still passes as a joke in the 'topfunnyjokes' website on the
Internet - one-liners-jokes/tell-woman-two-black-eyes*

# Metamorphosis

The air she moves through shivers silvery with fear,
Things seem slower, lights seem brighter, her hands are cold.
She's nervous, she keeps saying she's nervous,
'I'm so sorry I'm nervous' 'I'm so nervous' she says over and over.
As she fidgets on the couch, plaiting her fingers,
Pushing a strand of newly-dyed hair back behind her ear,
A small, round woman, no longer young,
Dragging her courage up,
Because she is in the magic place, the place of change,
A place she never thought she'd be in while she managed
And loved and tended others - husband, children, her old mum.

But now she wants something for herself, she wants the old her back
Not to be young, but to be herself, not someone's wife,
Someone's mother, her true name unsung, herself submerged,
And she wants to own that self again;
It doesn't take much to work the spell,
Just a little thing, a small tattoo, a sigil, a sign, a key
That unlocks herself to herself once more.
So she has a rose, a butterfly, that chalice of women's pain, Frida,
A goddess, a wild flower, a triple moon, a cat,
Nothing big and showy, no backpiece or oriental sleeve,
No ego, no shots for Instagram begging for *Likes*.

Instead she endures the ordeal quietly and unwinds
From the chrysalis of her years of love and sacrifice
And becomes free, in the needles' blood embroidery,
In the slow rhythm, the voluntary sacrifice of pain,
The ritual and the grace and she flies, she flies again.

*Joolz Denby*

# Scéimh

Stánaim orm féin,
Sa scáthán fada sa seomra folctha
Agus déanaim imscrúdú ar mo chorp
Nach bhfuil óg a thuilleadh,
Ar na cuair, na roic, na coilm,
Na cnapáin, na goiríní sofheicthe,
Na cúinní folaithe –
Gach boilsceann, gach meall, gach pluc.

Bhí an t-am ann
Nach raibh mé in ann amharc orm féin,
Lomnocht.
Ní raibh mé mar a d'inis na hirisí domh
Gur cheart a bheith.

Lapóg, déanta d'im agus d'uachtar na hÉireann,
Sprochaillí dubha faoi na súile,
Liopóga craicinn thuas agus thíos orm,
Agus an áit ar at mo bholg le páistí
Gur bhrúigh siad a mbealach amach
Ag pléascadh ar an tsaol.
Na créachtaí a d'fhág an máinlia
Mar ar sháigh sí a scian
Isteach i mo chuid feola,
Arís,
Is arís eile,
Thar na blianta.

Anocht, sa seomra folctha,

Mo chraiceann fliuch, sciúrtha, cumhra,

Tá mé chomh sásta le mo scéimh sa scáthán,

Beag beann ar shlupar-shlapar an tuáille,

Chomh sásta le mo chorp

A thóg tríd an tsaol seo mé,

Chomh sásta go bhfuil mé ann.


*Réaltán Ní Leannáin*

# Beauty

I stare at myself,
In the long mirror in the bathroom
I pore over my body,
No longer young,
I see the curves, the wrinkles,
The scars, the lumps and invisible bumps,
The hidden corners,
Every knot and bulge and pucker.

There was a time
I couldn't bear to see myself,
Undressed.
I wasn't how the magazines told me
I should be.

A squishy little woman, formed
From the cream and the butter of Ireland,
Black shadows under my eyes,
Fleshy rolls above and below,
Where my stomach swelled with children
Until they burst their way out
Exploding into the world.
The gashes that the surgeon left
Where she thrust her knife
Into my flesh

Again,
And again,
Through the years.

Tonight, standing at the bath tub,
My skin wet, scoured and fragrant,
I accept my beauty in the mirror,
Unheeding of the shlip-shlap of the towel,
So content with this body
That has brought me through life,
Happy to be alive.

*Réaltán Ní Leannáin*

# I am a woman

I am a woman.
I have short hair, my mother's eyes
And her button nose
I laugh like her
And sigh like her
I worry I'm becoming her

I am a woman.
When I was born
The doctor observed and declared
'Congratulations, it's a girl!'
She also said, 'She has her father's feet!'
I have always wondered,
How did she know what my father's feet looked like?

I am a woman.
I don't wax…anything
I like the sensation
Of a gentle breeze wafting the hairs on my legs.
Sometimes, I twiddle my armpit hair
While watching TV

I am a woman.
When my period started
I was so proud and embarrassed
My mum told my dad - 'Why did you do that?!'
He treated me differently from that moment on

I am a woman
I like eye shadow and mascara
I never got my head around lipstick –
It just keeps coming off!
Who has time to reapply?

I am a woman.
I was raped when I was fifteen
At a party

By a boy I'd only just met
I was drunk, and guilty
I shouldn't have even been there

I am a woman.
My first love was a sweet
And gentle boy of seventeen
He drove a blue pick-up and loved Metallica
He used to make me grilled cheese sandwiches
And had a cat he named 'bear'

I am a woman.
'Mines a pint of bitter, thanks.'
Sometimes I like a G&T
Others, a whiskey
And occasionally, a white wine spritzer

I am a woman.
I kissed a girl
And I liked it

I am a woman.
My favourite subjects in high school were:
Science
Maths
Sociology
English
Art
I hated P.E.
But I loved swimming and I hold a black belt in Jujitsu


I am a woman.
I have been pregnant six times
I have one living child
A beautiful boy
Who will one day be a beautiful man
I'm making sure of that


I am a woman.
I wonder sometimes
What does my caesarean scar look like
From the inside of my womb?


I am a woman.
I have flushed miscarried embryos down the toilet
I have had miscarried embryos sucked out of my body
I have held my dead daughter
In my hands
After pushing her, feet first, out of my vagina

I am a woman.
In my twenties, I wore 'men's cologne'
Because I liked it
Last year, I started wearing 'women's perfume'
Because I like it
(Psst…it's the same stuff.)

I am a woman.
I am a daughter, sister, niece, wife, MOTHER
I miss breastfeeding.
Even though I also hated it at times
I loved the mammalian nature of it
My mammalian nature

I am a woman.
I'm a pain in the ass
And I don't give a shit
What you think
…I do actually, a little bit

I am a woman.
I used to lift weights for strong muscles
A flat stomach
Toned legs
Now I have a soft belly
I am strong and soft
My life has been carved, moulded by this fact
Of biology
This body has given me great joys
And great pains

It carries me through it all
It will do so until I die

Still a woman

I know what I am.
Woman
Woman
Woman
Woman
It's all the label I ever want or need


*Moonbee*

# KISSES XX

I never asked to be like this, but I was born this way,
How I wished for something different, day after bloody day.
I wanted things I couldn't have, but no matter how I wished
Still every day I'd wake up to find I'm still like this.
The dresses and the dolls, I hated with a passion
Dungarees and wellie boots were much much more my fashion.


As an adult I could choose how I wished to live my life
So I made the right decision, I'd be no mother, nor a wife.
I'd live the life I wanted, and wear whatever I like
I'd go into construction, and yes, get called a dyke.
In time I made my peace with the sex I had been born
Thank God I'm not a child now 'cos I would be so torn.


The teachers they would tell me I should have been a boy
Just because I hated skirts and played with the wrong toy.
They'd pass me onto therapists who'd affirm that I was right
They'd tell me that my breasts could be bound all flat and tight.
The doctors would agree and then fill me full of pills
Persuaded that's the right course by the Pharma corporate shills.

Then finally the surgeon, who'd sworn to do no harm -
I'd get my breasts removed; make a penis from my arm.
All to live the life I wanted, and wear whatever I like
I'd have still been a builder, and still got called a dyke.
You are what you are born as. There is no changing sex.
It's as it always has been. Men are XY, and women XX.

*BoiledBeetle*

# Why they burnt the Maid

Not because
she cropped her hair short
short as a man's
Not because
she refused to wear frocks
but dressed like a man

Not because she slept alone
and not with a man

Not because
she rode a fine stallion
and bore a tall banner
and wore heavy armour
and beat them in battle
and fought like a man

Not because
she offended the Lord
did they brand her a witch
and set her aflame

But because
she dared do all this
and was not
a man

*Magi Gibson*

# A Prayer Before Being

Before I become what I am becoming
Before my decisions are set into stone
Before I begin to transition my meaning
             of fear into self, and
                      myself into bone
before I begin to transition

Keep me from kind people
the kind of people for whom lying is a kindness
who yearn to shield us from the truth, or
                      otherwise to blind us
who reckon their own righteousness is all they need
             to guide us

Keep me from kindly people
who, with a sort of mindless kindness, vouchsafe
                      my confusion
who prophesy in part, and so encourage
                      my delusion
who drive me to impose myself, and model it
                      inclusion

keep me from those who make kindness their cause
who hide cruel practice as making good law
who make me the frontline and strike up a pose
                      keep me from all those

I am not yet become all I shall be
Let not my doctors unbecome me
don't let my flesh become their possession
don't let my form become my obsession
       but let me survive and transcend my mistakes
and hide not the truth for my sake

Keep me from kind people
those who advance themselves through disruption
shills who denounce but practise corruption
whited sepulchres filled with old bones
             keep me from all those

and if I must choose between kindness and clarity
if my existence be threatened by fact
let me discern between madness and charity
let me desist with my courage intact

I am a changeling of promise and plea
I am a person of blood and of bones
Don't let the kind ones rearrange me
Keep me from all those.


*Sonya Douglas*

79

# She

She was not gender non-conforming.
She was not a girly-girl.
She was not a tomboy.
She was an ordinary girl.
She was very much loved.

She was smart.
She loved to read.
She loved her American Girl dolls.
She played soccer.
She played the violin.
She was very much loved.

She was kind and helpful.
She was a good friend.
She called her mother mommy – even as a teen.
She was a firstborn.
She was very much loved.

She had a favourite striped dress.
She had bright brown eyes.
She liked to visit the mall with her friends.
She loved to bake.
She was very much loved.

She became interested in animal welfare.
She became a vegetarian.
She asked permission to date a boy at age thirteen.
She purchased bras from Victoria's Secret
She began to spend more time on her computer.
She was very much loved.

She was bullied on social media by a boy.
She dreamed of winning a concerto competition.
She said she would wear a formal blue gown if she won.
She enrolled in a competitive honours program.
She received a smartphone on her birthday.
She was very much loved.

She came out as lesbian in high school.
She helped to form the GSA at her school.
She uncovered Tumblr on her smartphone.
She dreamed of attending an elite college.
She was sometimes hostile at home.
She was very much loved.

She accepted an offer to an elite college.
She became an activist in multiple causes.
She was immersed in an alternative Tumblr world.
She wore a strapless black dress to prom.
She engaged in black and white thinking.
She was very much loved.

She wasn't present even when she was present.
She went off to college.
She seemed okay for a while.
She was not okay.
She wasn't sleeping much.
She was faraway, far away from home.
She was very much loved.

She arrived home for a visit.
She had a queer demeanour.
She was very thin.
She wore a wispy moustache, baggy clothes.
She was always on her phone – not present.
She was very much loved.

She left home suddenly.
She did not return.
"She is killing herself. She is killing all of us!"
*(Said her mother collapsed on the floor.)*
She went dark on social media.
She refused contact with her family.
She was very much loved.

She made a trans pronouncement from afar.
She was prescribed testosterone at her college's health centre.
She changed her name – first and last names.

She had her breasts excised.

She is barely recognisable to those who have known and loved her.

She was very much loved.

She is loved.

*Rainey G.*

# TOPIARY

Yew
in the shape
of a pawn or a rook
at a push but not tall
enough to be king
or queen, we'd
have to wait
for yew
to grow
unclipped
freestanding,
but we're ready now
our secateurs sharp
to keep yew small. Our vision
Our Chessboard Our game.


*Liz Houchin*

# Identity

*identity*
did not force my lines
to curve

did not ease
the weight on load-bearing
arches

did not deconstruct
its own motivations when
there was nothing left to queer

did not
pin me down, unprovoked,
on an evening like any other

did not provide
the sovereignty
it had promised

or anything I could touch

*empowerment*
was a cruel tease,
flirting with me for decades

telling me
it was my own fault
when compromise failed

breaking my branches
when they reached out
for sunlight

selling
my half-formed silhouette back to me
as the whole woman

shadows
a collection of shapes
and parts

a pile of laundry

*Nicole Jones*

# You're Still a Woman

*For my daughter, for all of our daughters*


You're my size, you're still a woman.
   Always have been, always will be.
      You can't have forgotten?
Are you really hoping words and surgery
      Are big enough moves to change your reality?


I can't sit by and watch this, it's a travesty.
   I get you don't like your body
      And everything it signifies
But why base your entire personality
      On far-fetched goals and lies?
        *You're still a woman, my size.*


I know you hate to hear it
   And it makes you disassociate
      But when you're grown, you'll get it
And you'll regret all of this self-hate.


You're looking through a shitty lens
   The 'Glitter Family' gave you.
It's murky, scratched up
   And reused so much
      by their design
It won't let you see the real you –
*You're still a woman, my size.*

87

You're bigger, stronger and more real than them
   And they know this
      Which is why they want to keep you at your lowest.
'Found family' they'll also call it
     As they tear you from those who really love you.


The ones who love you for you just as you are – unlike them
I'm sorry, but they're... who?
   *You're still a woman, my size.*


You grew because of our sex class
   you're You
     Even while you're blinded by this farce
*You're still a woman, my size.*


                 *Anna Castle*

# Mum they say

Strong as a mother
tired as a mother
tied up as a mother

in impossible knots
between my heart
and my holes
between the past
and might never
between tomorrow
and death.

Playing with skulls
dicing up their eyes
rolling up my sleeves
counting all the crows
trying not to cry.

Birthing oceans
tsunamis of me
building up mountains
just to jump off a cliff.

*Mara Ricoy Olariaga*

# Walking Out

She finds she is beautiful, not in the world's way,
but in the walking sway of an older woman
solitary on an April dawn, passing fields

where rape flower smells of honey.
Fat black hens are out already, strut, peck
through an open garden, ignore her as she passes

in a loose blue skirt, shirt half done,
a shawl around her shoulders.
She can do little except proclaim

her rickety, strong tendons and parts,
allow the world to enter through pores, eyes,
heavy, softening breasts.

Hers at last, this sweet autonomy of flesh,
unshiftable now, her veins running warm.
She absently swipes at seedheads, ground elder,

takes the sandy path to a sea she has dreamt of,
time and time over in slow, heavy waves
flecked with sea-horses and minnows.

She wades in, blue skirt clinging, smells
charred wood from the sunken village
some say still smoulders below.

*Mary O'Donnell*

# Do not speak to me of pain

*a response to 'The Extraction of the Stone of Madness' by Hieronymus Bosch*


after my father died, i saw him everywhere.
driving the bus. in the hardware store discussing the unique
benefits of one lawn mower over another. waving at me
from coffin shaped clouds.


when i was trying to fall pregnant, all i saw were
pregnant women. some with one already in the pram. a second
toddling alongside the wheels. a third selfishly baking
in wombs fertilised with blood & bone.


now everywhere i look i see exhausted women.
this one in a yellowing field. a white knight-less horse in the
distance. fat red book on her head. red is her colour.
knowledge becomes her.


she looks on at the man banging on about
his pain. she listens. wilting like a garden of artichokes
planted too close to the frost. the drum of her heart, heavy
as a load of un-spun bath towels hauled from the washing
machine & hung on the line
never to dry.


the surgeon with the funnel on his head
(that no-one seems concerned about) makes his first incision.
*'I see this all the time,'* he says, hacking into the man's head
foraging for the stone of madness, *'particularly in men your age.*

*A very serious condition - far more painful than the inferor*
*woman-stone. I mean the average man-stone could easily render*
*a man unable to take out the bins, cook a meal—even feed the*
*oxen! Indeed, the best he could perhaps manage might be to*
*lift a tankard of ale to his very lips!'*

the woman slumps forward onto the
table that might topple if she leans too
hard. she is not used to leaning.

& it is not that she has no sympathy for the man.
just she's had her own lonely years of period pain, then the ovarian
cancer, the ovariectomy, the appendectomy, the hysterectomy & now
the diverticulitis that has appeared out of nowhere & there is talk
of a man with a funnel on his head removing
the diseased part of her colon.

but she will cross that moss covered bridge when
she comes to it. for now there are bins to take out, oxen to feed,
rabbits to stew - with or without artichokes, it will depend
on the crop.

& she knows her own stone of madness
is growing now too. taking up space in her head like her
dead mother's sideboard she did not want & now sits in her garage
gathering dust & guilt. but she will not have it removed.
she will learn to live with it.

it is what exhausted women do.

*Ali Whitelock*

# SO....

So, we are accused of hate:

It's true.
We do!

We hate men simply taking
We hate their vile faking
We hate the intrusion
We hate the delusion
We hate men dictating
We hate men fixating
We hate child abuse
We hate every excuse
We hate cheating in sport
We hate ads that distort
We hate being derided
We hate it's one-sided
We hate losing our right
We hate having to fight


We hate all right!

*Jean Livingstone*

# The Stand

Could you stand in honest truth
when all seems lost?
Could you face your unknown fate
and pay the cost?
When mad belief brings untold grief
and logic drowns,
could you meet their angry mob
and stare them down?

Could you stand when others fail
to put things right?
Could you face the government
with all their might?
When poison spreads to hearts and heads
disguised as good,
could you meet their biased courts
misunderstood?

Could you stand and try to help
when people hurt?
Could you face the ridicule
and smearing dirt?
When darkness lifts to show that cliff
do you turn back?
Could you meet the charging horde
and risk attack?

When you stand where others fail
it lifts their heart.
When you stand and hope prevails
their courage starts.
Momentum grows, this moment shows
you're not alone.
When reason stands and counts the crowd
then truth is known.

*L.P. French*

# Good Girl

I've learnt the way of strangers,
dangers in the dark,
games like patience, solitaire,
and words like patriarch.

I know my hiding places,
shoe size, weight and height,
the long way round, the short-cut,
a wrong think from a right.

I've memorised novenas,
all the school rules, lyrics. Yet
The reason for this vigilance
is harder to forget.

*Rachel Rooney*

# First Confession

The hard wood was sore
on my one unskint knee.
The priest's robes were white
and watercress green.

In my pew, in the queue,
I was neatly contrite,
my sins at the ready
and rounded to three.

I knew them by heart
but kept one unmentioned
(the one that had most chance
of scuppering heaven) –

the boy in my garden
unzipping his fly,
boring the snake
through the gape of his hands,

saying *tell who you like,*
*they'll never believe you* −
even at seven
he knew his best weapon.

So I told them nothing
of eyeing a godhead,
wondering if God felt
a prick on his conscience.

On the drive home from church
I got to sit in the front,
take the penance of big girls
and be really grown-up.

*Julie Sheridan*

# Thirteen

First blood
a stain
on baby blue
brushed cotton sheets

the shame

I leaked

red rose folded over
in bed clothes closed
to hide

my secret withering
to brown inside

Each moon
I bleed

some flashes
seep deeper

reach the mattress

for months
my sheet (unchanged
because of shame)

dirty
ripped
and threadbare in my bed

entangles my legs
in ribboned shreds.


*Colette Colfer*

# A Bit of Fun

'It was just a bit of fun,' he said.
'We were having a laugh.'

As I sobbed over
the state-of-the-art Casio
that was just like my dad's,
its face broken, the glass
shattered as I lashed out
in self-defence.

The teacher, shame-faced,
silently took my watch.

And replaced the glass.

Other things
are less easily
repaired.

*Mairi Cameron*

# Scar

In summer we gingerly pushed back stinging
nettles, carefully held down the rusting
barbed-wire with a stick and one by one climbed
over. My turn, the boy ahead let go
too soon. The silver-coloured barb snapped back
pierced my thigh and I cried to the boys' jeers
then saw the inch long tear, dark blood
spilling from my groin —
soiling my sky-blue shorts.

I unhooked myself from the lethal wire,
tried to stanch the flow with dock leaves.
Almost fifty years later, I recall
that afternoon as I step from my shower,
see the silvery scar on my skin
and think how that day was almost an end
of innocence, an early spilling of blood.

My shame at my spoiled shorts, the jeering boys
setting me apart,
marked female.

*Jean O'Brien*

# Violated

I remember when I
was scared to be
myself

But they decided
they wanted all of
me anyway.

They took it.

*Emily*

# Seven Dwarves

One had anger issues
and he blamed them all on me.

One stayed in his bedroom
so we met infrequently.

One was always grinning
yet he couldn't tell a joke.

One was word allergic.
kept on sneezing when I spoke.

One seemed keen. He flirted
but he failed to make a pass.

One looked cute (and stupid).
he got worse when smoking grass.

One believed in healing
though he never wrote a note.

Now I'm lying in a glass box
with an apple down my throat.

*Rachel Rooney*

# Dead. Women. Count.

She counts dead women. Not women
wiped out in warzones by bullets and bombs, nor
the 63 million missing in India - Rita Banjeri
is keeping count of them. Nor is she counting

the Korean Comfort Women, piecing
together what's left of their bones
in the fire pits where they perished. No,
she keeps count closer to home. Not just

the victims of those wild-eyed strangers they drilled
us to evade: *stay with your pals when you leave the pub,*
*don't walk down darkened lanes, don't take shortcuts*
*through woods alone, don't get into vans,*

*don't wear too short skirts, too high heels,*
*low-cut tops, don't end up a headline*
*a corpse a break-a-mother's-heart statistic in a ditch.*
Not, not just those! She is counting women

killed with knives, shotguns, ropes, with septic
tanks and fists, with poison, cricket bats and fire
each killed by a man who said he loved her once,
a boyfriend, husband, partner, ex, a man she trusted

in her home. A man who thought her life
no longer counts. But she is counting,
every week, every one.
And we are counting with her.

*Magi Gibson*

# Instructions for Excising the Bad Man

*"Frankly, by the time the police show up to arrest a bad man, the damage has usually already been done." The Guardian, 7 October 2021*

To start: bring the scalpel
as close as you can to your eyeball.
This calls for forensic focus.
Bald your mind of all recall.
Picture yourself upturning the pencil,
erasing the letter to the TV presenter
your mother urged you to script.
(Don't expect a pony.
Nothing will be fixed.)
Scissor past every scene
that you've ever seen
of a man with his hands at his groin.
(First day at school, alone on the bus,
or thirteen on a 5am paper-run. Keep going.)
Gulp in big breaths
of mephitic anaesthetic.
Exhale. Excise. Expunge.
Oblige without question
when the friend you're driving
asks you to skip that song.
(Instruct your adolescent self
to take his posters off the wall.)

You could keep on cutting
but the art of a surgeon
is knowing when time's up.
Apply the cauter, hotter, holler,
suture and compress.
In fact, while you're at it
unstitch the white dress
and for god's sake cancel the castle.
Stash a packet of maggots
up your sleeve at all times
or in your nearest pocket.
(Reserve for the truly necrotic).
To the light of these sundry
debridement devices
now orient the scar.
What do you do if it weeps?
Darling, go back to the start.

*Julie Sheridan*

# My Right Fist

Left leg forward, right leg back

Jab, jab                unapologetic
Cross hook                      look out, world
Upper cut                       my weight behind it

Jab, jab
Correct my stance.
Pivot from the hip.

Majik – and yes, that is his name,
This trainer half my age,
Majik keeps shuffling backwards.
I? I advance.
My padded fist connects. I love that smack!

Left leg forward, right leg back,
Correct – again – my stance.
Light on my feet,
Bounce, bounce.

Jab, jab.
Upper cut.
Upper cut.

My strong right fist
When it lands true
With all my weight behind it
Then leaps up to guard my face
And gives my weaker left its chance.

Cross. Jab.
DANCE.

*Victoria Whitworth*

# Scríob bean

Scríob bean, faigh dearg
dearg na fola, fuil na feirge, fearg fir, fir fiata, faobhar paisin
teasaíocht cuimilte, cuimilt craicinn, craiceann dearg, craiceann nua
cneá chiúin, nuabeirthe,
fiántas instinne
fanacht slán
sábháilte.
Scríob bean.

# Scratch a woman

Scratch a woman, find red
the red of blood, the blood of anger, the anger of men, ferocious men,
razor sharp passion
heat soothed, skin caressed, red skin, new skin
quiet wounds, newly born,
the savagery of instinct
staying safe
and sound.
Scratch a woman.

*Réaltán Ní Leannáin*

# For Mary

*Mary Gordon 12/9/68 - 8/3/23*


we give you
seven hills, sisters
reclined, women's banners
slung between
their breasts, a hammock
for your ease

we give you
leith sunshine
violet haar, a cloak
for blithe dissent
smirr, a benediction
for your ribbons

we give you
a queen's crossing
six white harps
thrumming with norland light
strummed by norland wind
for your ear's joy

we give you
a boat, unmoored
from a roof

a silver hull of mussel-shell
a fire-haired selkie warrior, prowed
for your setting forth

sister, we give you
a skein of beating wings
tips in the upwash
heading to the sea
lifting calling holding their v
as in love, as in a cup raised
for our, your victory


*Lorna Irvine*

# For Women's Rights

*(to the tune of Auld Lang Syne)*

We stand together side by side,
we will defend our rights.
We stand together side by side,
we'll not give up this fight.

For women's rights are human rights,
we won't let you forget.
For women's rights are human rights,
this isn't over yet.

Politicians and their friends may think
we can be cowed
Our minds and bodies we'll defend,
our NO will ring out loud.

For women's rights are human rights,
we won't let you forget
For women's rights are human rights,
this isn't over yet.

So gie's a hand in sisterhood,
our sex won't be denied
For dignity, reality,
we are standing side by side

For women's rights are human rights,
we won't let you forget
For women's rights are human rights,
this isn't over yet.


*Lucy Hunter Blackburn*

# Cataclysm

Later that night, we took her
body back, held her close.
We bathed her peeled skin, wrapped
her flesh in soft cloth.
Her face, her beautiful face.
Not a hair left, the violence still
seen in the hollows of her eyes.
We saw the pain of her slow death,
consumed, gagged, her legs bone
from the knee down.

In the morning light, we ran home
across the hills to our baby girls, to
clutch them and whisper spells into
their tiny ears, prophecies hurled
through generations:

We will name our bodies
We will name our experience
We are the women
We are the sisters

We are the mothers
We are the daughters
We are the granddaughters
of the witches
you did not burn.

*Arwen Webb*

# Wildling

You cannot tame this wildling lass,
my feelings rage, my thoughts are vast.
The future calls and though the past
is part of me,
no one controls my wayward soul
for I am free.

*L.P. French*

# This Is For Us

This is for all the bad victims
For the gobby bitches
For the girls who wouldn't stay down
For the women who fought back
For the tattooed and the tearaways
The ones with sullen eyes
The ones who can't speak about it
The women who didn't know
They were supposed to take notes
The human women who cried
Hot tears of rage and frustration
Who weren't dainty or diminutive
Who raised their eyes
Who hung on by their fingernails
Who asked for help
And were escorted from the premises
Who stood with their children
Behind them when he screamed
Don't raise your fucking fists to me
For the women scarred for life by life
For the women who drank
To stop the dreams
To the girls who bled
Silently in the bathroom
The savage blossoms
Of a long dark night

This is for all of us who did
The wrong thing
Who paid the price
Who refused to lie
Who lived despite it all.

This. Is. For. Us.

*Joolz Denby*

# Lilith

I'd had enough so I stood
on a tussock outside the house,
shouted the *hashem hameforash*
loud as a curse, felt a tickle
at my shoulder blades, the first
feathers sprout, an eruption
of wing cascading into cloak.

I stroked the air, flexing to test
the stretched-out span, lifted up
poised in passé en relevé
as my husband ran
the path from the porch
and grasped at my ankles
to anchor me back
but I slipped like smoke
into the smiling sky
and at last was above him,
surfing thermals and the Coriolis force.

I knew tapestries would be woven
depicting me as demonic for leaving,
later heard stories
of me strangling newborns,
having sex with demons.

They said I was the black moon,
succubus, riding the night,
tracing the sweet scent of chaste young men
to straddle and steal their semen.
They called my babies Lilin,
and for protection strung amulets
with angels' names
on the necks of their children.

I didn't care what they said
and laughed at their lies.
Now I had flight and truth and freedom.

*Colette Colfer*

# I cannot go on (said the otter) I cannot go on

cradling my pup on the raft of my body,
stripping the striated muscle from the spine
of the quick-finned fish I caught between my paws.

I cannot go on catching. I cannot go on chirruping
and sliding down the mudchute beside the river,
I cannot cradle my pup on the raft of my body.

I cannot cradle my pup on the raft of my body
(the wet warm-pelted raft of my body,
the loving raft, the water-rocked raft of my body)

(my pup, here is my pup, whom I cannot go on cradling)

knowing what otters do. I cannot unknow
(turn aside now, if you want to go on cradling
your perfect pup on the welcome raft of your body)

unknow that otters (some otters, other otters,
not all otters, we otters) rape seal pups and their corpses,
pounding and groping the rotten meat apart
until it escapes them in the stinking river.

How can I cradle or play or chirrup?
How do I lie like a raft on the brilliant water
even with my pup, my perfect pup,
and the wide bright day, and the sky?

*Anon 1*

124

# let me eat cake and go quietly to seed

in this age of positive thinking
and mani-fucking-festation may i complain
proudly & publicly of ageing & all things
bodily. may i wax lyrically of my now un-
obstructed bowel, trumpet joyously to the
world of my failing eyes & drooping breasts
my liver spots & hearing loss, my increased
cholesterol & hypertension

may i no longer feel obliged to appear
positive in the face of my increased
risk of heart disease, may we stop calling
fucked up situations challenges & stop
looking for reasons bad things happen—
there are none

may i never sport elastane cycling shorts,
fluorescent orange jogging shoes & t-shirts
that urge the reader to never never never give
up with the font size increasing like you are
climbing the arrochar alps one jagged peak
at a time

may i never carry a water bottle—let me risk
dehydration from the house to the bus stop

how i am tired of counting my blessings
& watching my waist line—please just let me
eat cake & go quietly to seed

may i continue to enjoy bearing unnecessary
grudges & curl up here on the couch to watch
christopher hitchens denounce god on YouTube

may i climb the paps of jura to sing the
praises of the breast cancer i do not yet have
& the ovaries that once held hope

may i tell of my gratitude for the cervix that
no longer needs to be papped nor smeared, of
my aching fingers & swollen joints—how i
can barely squeeze the sponge into the corner
of my loaf tin to dislodge the baked on dough

must i listen to the woman on the train platform
vomit her opinion on refugees & the white teacher
talk of her surprise when the black kid bled red. must i worry the pains
in my chest at midnight mean i'm having a heart attack. must i tell the
doctor my nails are softer since she told me to stop eating cheese

must i now check the density of my bones
make appointments i cannot be bothered making
must they send me invitations to mammograms
& dental checks but never to champagne &
nibblies

how i like to hear noise. how i like to make it
how they take the eggs from the battery hen
but do not stop to hear her song. how i hear
he is raping his step daughter now. how
silence restricts your wings. how you never
wanted to fly anyway.


*Ali Whitelock*

# I don't know what to do with all the rage

I don't know
what to do with all the rage.
I have tried burying it,
but lost sleep over the guilt.
I have tried to outrun it,
but couldn't keep up the pace.
I have tried putting it aside,
but it stared at me from my bookshelf.
I have tried doing the reading,
but that only left me with more questions.
I have tried asking the questions,
but couldn't hear the answers over all the noise.
I have tried writing a formal letter of complaint,
but received a copy-paste reply.
I have tried writing elsewhere,
but the record disappeared.
I have tried taking a photograph,
but its face was impenetrable.
I have tried matching the expression,
but I didn't like the person I became.
I have tried building with it,
and it's the only thing that's worked so far.


*Nicole Jones*

# #WhatIsAWoman

*Dedicated to my sister, Netha Islam. Netha lived from*
*08/02/71 - 07/08/21 and died of ovarian cancer.*


I am not a hairstyle
I am not a dress
I am not makeup
I am not breasts
I am not a vulva
I am not a waist
I am not a smell
I am not a taste
I am not periods
I'm not even birth
I don't need their approval
To know my worth.


I am not a saint
I am not a whore
I am simply female
I need nothing more.
I am not a hormone level
I'm not a hobbled man
Just like Rachel's not black
Cos she got herself a tan.

I am not a feeling
I am not a trend
I'm a Goddamned angry woman
Who needs this shit to end.

Forget all their rules about what little girls can do
There's no wrong way to be a woman,
There's no wrong way to be you.
Adult is gender neutral,
But they mean the same,
Woman just means female
Of a certain fucking age.

*Serena Partrick*

# They told me I was a ... Ciswoman

I asked what cis meant.
They said, Ciswomen feel no mismatch between
their biological sex and their gender identity

They say, It's Latin, as though it were
the Word of God. They say it's just an adjective
(actually, it's a prefix)

They say, It's not a slur...
It is a slur. It's a slap in the face
It's a scold's bridle

They say, It's just the opposite of trans
Cis women, stay in your lane
You have no monopoly on womanhood

Cis gasps in a too-tight corset
Cis totters on too-high heels
Cis calls her make-up her 'face'

and won't leave the house without it
Ciswomen feel no mismatch between
their biological sex and their gender identity

No speedbumps or potholes
or square pegs in round holes
Ciswomen flow effortlessly

from childhood into womanhood.
No need for de Beauvoir, no painful "becoming",
just sleep-waltzing into full femininity

Ciswomen KNOW what to do with their hair!
No effort, no burden, no caricature,
it's never a drag – it's just who they ARE...

Because they're worth it
Ciswomanhood is never pushed on girls
by advertising, by magazines, by Tiktok

and Tumblr, by mothers fearful of what happens
to girls who don't "girl" properly, by fathers, who
approve of pretty, compliant girls

Real Ciswomen "Feel like a woman" 24/7
HOW EXHAUSTING. Always on show,
if only to yourself

Skimpy clothes, high heels, make up,
dieting, gossip, doing other women down
How can Ciswomen be friends with each other?

Form alliances? Build a movement?
Ciswomen LOVE the chains that bind them
IT WAS BAD ENOUGH

when the Ciswoman was Virgina Woolf's
"looking glass possessing the magical
and delicious power of reflecting the figure

of man at twice his natural size"
IT WAS BAD ENOUGH
when the Ciswoman was Betty Friedan's

smiling middle-class housewife,
her brains curdling with boredom.
No wonder, in this sadistic porn-sick world

we have not built, we are ordered to be Ciswomen.
When #chokemedaddy is a Twitter hashtag,
a schoolyard catch-phrase...

IT WAS BAD ENOUGH - BUT NOW?
Ciswomen feel no mismatch between
their biological sex and their gender identity

Ciswomen feel no mismatch between their
biological sex and their performance of femininity
No mismatch between their biological sex and their

drag act between their biological sex
and their oppression
So, maybe you're a happy

"Cisgendered man"?
Happy celebrating your place at the top
of the hierarchy, shouting women down,

silencing us, ignoring us.   Fine!   You do you.
But we won't shut up and we won't lie down
We are not your magic mirror

We are not your support humans
We are not your toys
We are not ciswomen

We are women.

*Victoria Whitworth*

# There was an old woman...

There was an old woman who swallowed a lie
I don't know why she swallowed a lie
Perhaps she'll die

There was an old woman who swallowed a fad
That a girl who liked football was really a lad
She swallowed a fad to prop up the lie
I don't know why she swallowed the lie
Perhaps she'll die

There was an old woman who gave up her words
She promised to use only pronouns preferred
She called herself cis, she thought it was kind
It wasn't enough, now she's lost her mind

There was an old woman who gave up her spaces
Now she's cycling with men
who win all of the races
She gave up her spaces to prop up the lie
I don't know why she swallowed the lie
Inside she'll die

There was an old woman who lost all her rights
For the sake of some men
who wear lacy black tights
She lost all her rights to prop up the lie
I don't know why she swallowed the lie
Inside she'll die

Then up spoke some women who said
we won't lie
And this is the hill on which we will die
You won't take our spaces,
you can't have our rights
Cos truth is our weapon
and we'll win this fight.

*Rebecca Heath*

# A working week

Week in, week out at meetings:
gender ideology,
gender ideology,
gender ideology,
gender ideology,
gender ideology,
gender ideology.

My ears hurt, my eyes roll,
my stomach lurches.
Is anyone else as visibly cringed out as I?
No alternative view would be allowed.
I sit silent,
I feel a coward,
I have no real power.
To challenge is isolation,
a battle I cannot take on.

This is:
the blind leading the blind,
the woke virtue-signalling,
the be kind being "kind".
Like sheep.

Maybe sheep are more thoughtful.

*Anna Fearon*

# Words behind flowers

It was fascinating,
extraordinary,
how quickly we moved
back into the shadows,
how we knew exactly what to do,
a place for everything,
and everything in its place,
our words behind flowers,
books turned in, spineless,
and the howls of rage
that came for them,
and the lies,
none of it, not a single bit,
ever a surprise.

*Anon 2*

# Anatomy of a Hounding

this split head throb, this frowning pate,
eyes soaked in sorrow, sleepless nights,
this smoking pout, grim row of teeth
sucking sepia through to lungs pulled tight
this bloated vision, this scrolling through
endless panic-inducing text,
this captured throat, this lumpen joke,
this complete and utter fucking mess.


this calm response through gritted gnashers,
heid kept while fingers rage out letters
this gut-swirl sick, this thud-burst heart
this hurting soul, frank, drunk, blood-letting,
this unhugged body, its every organ
debated bit by bit by bit,
but yer never allowed to be whole and sexed
(would ruin the fun to mention it.)


well, fuck this rightly, fellow houndees,
let's paint the town with colours bright,
bring all the verses and tales of righteous
opposition—and yes, bring wine.
let's soothe out furrows, bury sorrows,

refuse life in joyless, thankless fiction
no more caricatures, no more wracking bones
a life lived in truth is a beautiful mission.


*Jenny Lindsay*

# The Schism Ring

There Will Be Cake!
at the feminist literary gathering—
and tea and biscuits! and
gluten-free and vegan options!
exclamatory sprinkles and
safety warnings
in case of fire announcements
and Formica tables
and ghastly lighting
and a recognition and
a catering for everybody
covered and
uncovered by all topics listed!

     ... ...

Sometimes—
(and I admit this
in full knowledge of
all the ways it is
problematic)
I wish for a banquet
of frogs' legs, duck eggs and steak -
piles of mashed potatoes laden
with full fat butter and bacon—
the setting a dimly lit cavernous hall—
flagons of ridiculously expensive
craft ales that we've chored
from some dickhead bar
and I wish for a

big fuck-off boxing ring—
(non-lethal, fully accessible) *
designed for pillow fights
to sort out our differences.
We'll call it
The Schism Ring
and just as now
a match will be declared
but who cares who wins!
because
afterwards we'll devour chicken wings
and mozzarella buns
smothered in the hottest of hot sauce!
We'll get merry on bottles of malbec
and shout
FUCK YOUR BIOLOGICAL ESSENTIALISM!!
WELL—FUCK YOUR GENDER ESSENTIALISM!!
And then we'll hug
with these different
chests and breasts squishing
together in at least tacit understanding,
if not love...

Oh, folks, are we not bored of
angry Twitter sneers
and bigot calls
and hatred assumptions?
Tired of pouty faux-doe selfies
and Fuck The Patriarchy tote bags,
Such manicured, manufactured
resistance?

Women under thirty calling
their older sisters irrelevant witches
after all that they have done for us
IS MAKING ME VERY HUNGRY
for a family feast of reconciliation
not agreement, no—
a hearty banquet though,
not a polite, wee, agreeable cupcake.

Oh! I'm sorry. Eep! I'm sorry,
I am sosososososososo sorry...

D'ye think this is too masculine?
As I devour meat on the bone with bare hands?
Well, I'll not use cutlery or wipe my face silent when
judged by other criteria from men.

I'll fail no tick-box exercise in purity—
demure purity is the wrong ingredient,
unless we're wanting
egged face
flans sunk
cakes deflated
in the kitchen.

So, bring your lemon drizzle,
your rocky road,
your red velvet.
Bring your banana bread
and marshmallows.

And please do—please do
call me a misogynist.
This verse is dripping
with their damn stuff.
(It's very calorific...)
And I am one—at times—
and so are you:
we're fighting a system we are part of,
not individual atoms.

So, bring your ripened, arrogant plum puds,
your nippy wee ginger biscuits,
your thirsty tongues,
your razor wit sliced intae sixes
by all things listed.
Bring fistfuls of chocolate-cookie crust
and melting, childhood strawberry ices

Bring your loathing—
self and otherwise—
Bring your love.

Bring your love.

*Jenny Lindsay*

*The Schism Ring is also open to food fights and
most importantly—all are welcome.*

# Bridget Cleary's last message to her friend in the film production company

Well done :)
on saving yourself an appearance before
the House Un-American Activities Committee, Goody!

And sure,
it's only one wee Irish island's film festival
(and its female director) that you had to preemptively condemn.

I'm convinced
that in a couple of years you'll still be able to

boast about this…

*Estelle Birdy*

# To the women

Here's to the women who stand
The women who take their lives in their hands
Who hold to the truth on point of pain
Who are told they're insane and to stay in their lane
Here's to the women who still speak out
The women who say, speak, scream and shout
to make their voices heard
I know there's safety in silence
But you know that doesn't protect you from violence
Here's to the women who fight
The women with foresight
The women who teach
And each of you expounding, expanding her reach
So that others can fight
Here's to the women who know their worth,
And what their sisters are worth
Who birth daughters for warriors with only their words
And who step down from pedestals
Who rise up from doormats
Who hang their full weight from barred windows
And count reps while making their plans
Here's to those women
Here's to the women who stand.

*Sonya Douglas*

146

# By the end of June the earth was flat again

we stood mute at the deckle edge / our voices cut at the end
of the age of argument when all was said and nothing

the hopeful peered over tilting an ear to the black for the bounce
of pennies and tennis balls / the sound of the end of empty

the believers held hands and jumped as the final proof
they could fly / the lie remained unwinged and now

damp toes scuttled back, the shoreline pulping with tears
falling away / falling like wet snow at night

children wrote their names on cockled rocks with the nib
of a sharp stone / noughts and crosses scratched the truth

we watched them play and felt the gravity of want / they asked
who had curved the world, the question stung our eyes

then a plea to those we called witches for warning we were wrong:
*see that we are ready now! Revive the artists we flattened with the earth*

we curved their fractured fingers around charcoal and chalk
pressed to a birch peel nailed to a flitch of oak

and prayed in single silence for the skill to hatch and shade
for the gift to sketch a globe / for the wit to let it spin

*Liz Houchin*

# Contributors

**Aja The Empress** is an activist and poet who writes about the reality of sex in a world that dare not speak its name. After her first poem went viral, she used her voice to advocate for women and encouraged them to speak about the impact of transgender ideology on women's sex-based rights.

**Anon 1** is a professional author who, having already experienced personal hostility and bullying after expressing feminist views, does not want to reveal her real name. Although her work has always contained a strong feminist mindset, she has become more aware and more vocal about women's and children's rights after recently becoming a mother.

**Anon 2** is a nearly middle-aged writer and mum. She is dismayed by the curtailment of women's ability to express themselves politically and culturally, so this poem is for any woman unable to put her own name to her voice.

**Estelle Birdy** is a writer, book critic, yoga teacher and mother of four, living in Dublin. Her debut novel *Ravelling* has been optioned for TV and will be published in Spring 2024. Her short stories and poems have been shortlisted in competitions and published in journals and anthologies. A staunch anti-authoritarian she's been involved in women's rights activism for many years. Fizzy water is destroying her teeth.

**Lucy Hunter Blackburn** worked as a civil servant in Scotland before leaving to become a freelance researcher and study for a PhD. In late 2018, concerned at how government and public bodies were replacing sex with identity in law and policy, she formed policy analysis collective MurrayBlackburnMackenzie (MBM) with Lisa Mackenzie and Kath

Murray. She gifted *For Women's Rights* to the activist organisation For Women Scotland. The song was sung by women outside the Scottish Parliament as the Gender Recognition Bill was being passed on 22nd December, 2022.

**Boiledbeetle** As a victim of CSA Boiledbeetle has lifelong anonymity, so uses a pseudonym to keep her identity protected. As for Boiledbeetle, she explains: 'Summer 1976 aged four, whilst pretending to be an upturned beetle I was asked if I was a girl beetle or a boy beetle. A boiled beetle, I replied.'

**Brandubh** is a 14 year old secondary school student in Ireland who has come to prominence on social media for speaking out about gender ideology indoctrination in her school. The resultant bullying she has experienced has done nothing but strengthen her resolve to fight for the rights of women and girls. She is on Twitter - @brandubh4.

**Mairi Cameron,** 53, moved to Scotland in 1994 and will never leave! Former goth, former software engineer, organiser with the Scottish Feminist Network, founding member of the Forth Valley Feminists and always proud to stand up for women's rights

**Marisa Campbell** is an American ex-pat from the South Shore of Massachusetts. She emigrated to Scotland in 2013 and lives in Portobello, Edinburgh, with her husband and young sons. Her work has appeared in *Poetry Scotland, Blue Unicorn, and Euphony.*

**Anna Castle** is an autistic, half Romani mum of five, one of whom has Rapid Onset Gender Dypshoria (ROGD) and two who also have autism. She's currently deferred from doing her BSc Combined STEM at university because of losing her dad to glioblastoma. She recently fled DV. But she's thriving from finding a world of amazing, strong, brave and supportive women. Anna is taking legal action with another ROGD mum to challenge the lack of safeguarding and consistency in Adult Gender Clinic Service specifications, following on from the Cass Review for child gender clinics in the UK.

**Polly Clark** is the author of the novels *Larchfield* (2017) and *Tiger* (2019) and four poetry collections. Her work has been shortlisted for or won several awards including the TS Eliot Prize, Scottish Novel of the Year and Eric Gregory Award. '*Women*' won the 2004 MsLexia Poetry Prize judged by Selima Hill and appears in her collection *Take Me With You* (Bloodaxe, 2005). She is currently completing her third novel, *Ocean*.

**Colette Colfer** from County Wexford in Ireland is a lecturer in world religions. She previously worked in journalism and has won national awards for her radio documentaries. Colette was a runner-up in the Patrick Kavanagh Poetry Award 2019 and has had poems published in many publications.

**Joolz Denby** has been a professional award-winning novelist, visual artist and poet for over 45 years. She has toured the world with her writing and is an internationally collected artist, receiving a Gold Record from EMI for her iconic album cover for *New Model Army's Thunder & Consolation*. She owns and runs a boutique tattoo studio with an international clientele. Joolz has drawn on her own experiences of severe domestic and sexual trauma to research and fight for female victims and survivors of domestic and sexual abuse. She is known for her uncompromising stance on safeguarding for women and children.

**Dis_critic** began tying suffragette-coloured ribbons round lampposts, bus stops, anything that would stand still in Scotland in 2019. The aim was to get word out to women that their rights to same-sex services and spaces were being threatened. She remains anonymous to protect the dignity and privacy of her disabled daughter for whose right to same-sex care she fights in the face of a government who refuse to recognise her, and all women's, full humanity. She created the slogan *Women Won't Wheesht* to articulate her unwavering resistance to her daughter's boundaries being breached.

**Louise Distras** is a singer-songwriter from Wakefield whose spiky melodies and unvarnished lyrics won her praise from Kerrang! and BBC Radio 1. Her new album *'Beauty After Bruises'* is about womanhood and honouring the parts of ourselves that we look away from.

**Sonya Douglas** is an artist/writer/campaigner who advocates going back to first principles to establish basic truths on which you can rely in difficult times. Her motto is *Maintain your Boundaries*. She lives in Cardiff with her husband and daughter.

**Katherine Duffy** is an Irish poet based in Dublin. Her books include *Sorrow's Egg* (The Dedalus Press, 2011), and *Talking the Owl Away* (Templar Poetry, 2018), winner of Templar Poetry's Iota Shot Pamphlet award. She has given readings in Dublin, London, Paris, and in her beloved home town of Dundalk.

**Emily** writes for all the women who can't.   She says, "I speak for the women who are silenced. A brief and frank insight into losing yourself. Women are whole as they are and cannot be halved by another's words or actions. So, I write for all the women who can't."

**Anna Fearon** is an artist, writer, and feminist (of course). She found solace in feminism after suffering male violence and has never looked back. Anna uses Twitter to raise awareness of domestic abuse and has written about her personal experiences for FiLiA's blog and *Independent Voices*. Website: annafearonart.com

**Sharon Frame** is a 46 year old mum of three living in Glasgow and is currently a full time carer to her autistic son. She discovered a love of poetry after a trauma six years ago, and it has seen her through sad times and glad times.

**L. P. French**, also known as Suffragette Penny, is a passionate women's rights campaigner from Scotland and the poet for *Women Won't Wheesht*. She created the Terven Tuppence, an Pingin Saoirse and the Tuppenny Medal of Valour. They've the definition of woman stamped on them - adult human female. She's also a psychologist and an erratic collector of hobbies.

**Rainey G.** is a poet writing from the Pacific Northwest in the United States. She believes that poetry is a natural way of communicating our humanity. She dedicates this poem to her daughter, who opted out of womanhood.

**Rebecca Heath** is a 58 yr old recently retired lesbian primary school teacher, just moved to beautiful North Wales. She taught creative writing, art & drama and finds it very satisfying to use poetry in her women's rights activism.

**Liz Houchin** lives in Dublin. *Anatomy of a Honey girl (poems for tired women)* was published by Southword in 2021. In 2023 she was the Poetry Ireland poet-in-residence at the Scottish Poetry Library. Her work is supported by the Arts Council of Ireland.

**Lorna Irvine** Edinburgh-born and biding mother and civil celebrant, has worked in education, theatre and libraries; most happily of all, freelance-teaching in heritage sites and primary schools. A struggler with semi-permanent writer's-block, until events overwhelm, the sudden illness and death of creative voyager, campaigner and sister-friend, Mary Gordon, moved her to make her this parting gift.

**Nicole Jones** is an artist and writer born in Cornwall and currently based in Edinburgh. As a photographer, her work covers portraiture and event documentary, for clients including J. K. Rowling, Elaine Miller, and the campaign group Sex Matters. As a commentator, she has contributed to outlets such as *Channel 4*, *BBC Radio 1*, and *The Critic Magazine*. Her artistic practice and creative writing largely explore themes of female embodiment.

**Jenny Lindsay** is a poet, performer, essayist and literary events programmer based in Ayrshire, Scotland. She won the inaugural John Byrne Award for Critical Thinking in 2020 for her film-poem *The Imagined We*. The poems in this book are from her second collection *This Script*, which is also a poetry stage-show of the same name. She has been described as 'defiant, eloquent and inspiring' by *The Scotsman*.

**Jean M Livingstone.** Never, at the age of seventy did Jean think she'd be protesting outside the Scottish Parliament. Like many, she had been totally unaware that women's rights were in danger. Ever since, she's tried to do her bit. She's delighted to be included here amongst kindred spirits.

**Moonbee** is a psychotherapy student who has watched in horror as her profession has thrown women and children under the bus in the name of so-called 'inclusion'. She writes using a pseudonym as it's been made clear by her training institution and accrediting body that holding gender critical beliefs could cost her her livelihood. This is Moonbee's first published piece of work, and she is so proud to be amongst such wonderfully brave and talented women.

**Réaltán Ní Leannáin** publishes poetry, short stories and novels in Irish. She was part of the European Otherwords Project in 2016, was the 2019 Writer-in-Residence in Dublin City University and held the Dublin UNESCO City of Literature Irish Language Residency in 2021.

**Jean O'Brien**'s sixth and latest collection, *Stars Burn Regardless* was published by Salmon Poetry (Irl) 2022. She is an award winning poet, having won the Arvon International and the Fish International and been placed in many others. She was the 2021 Poet in Residence in the Centre Culturel Irlandais in Paris and awarded a Kavanagh Fellowship in 2017/18. One of her poems was recently put to music and choir by the New Dublin Voices and performed in Trinity College, Dublin, Ireland.

**Mary O'Donnell**'s work is often cited as key in expanding the horizons of Ireland's traditionally male-dominated literary world. She has published eight poetry collections, four novels and three short story collections. As a teacher of creative writing, her interest is in the forms, practices and critical reception of contemporary literature. *"It Wasn't a Woman"* and *"On Metaphor"* were published in her Salmon collection, *Massacre of the Birds*. *"Walking Out"* will appear in the chapbook *Outsiders, Always*, being Southword Editions, Cork. She is a member of the artists' affiliation Aosdana. www.maryodonnell.com

**Mara Ricoy Olariaga** is a survivor, a birth educator, a mother of three humans, a writer, activist, interpreter and proud feminist at FiLiA. She has also recently published a poetic feminist autobiography in Spanish called *Pendientes*.

**Abigail Ottley** writes poetry and short fiction. These poems come from her four times shortlisted but still unpublished pamphlet, *Pink Kimono*. An older woman, Abigail sees herself as both a survivor and a fighter. Born to a working-class home on the edge of East London, she lives in Penzance.

**Serena Patrick** is a 39 year old woman from Cornwall. Reading and writing poetry has been part of her life from a very early age. To Serena, words are the most marvellous tools; world-shaping, universe-explaining, soul-revealing tools of the utmost versatility, and she believes all human success stems from our capacity for language.

**Kathryn Robertson**'s day job is copywriting and slaying corporate jargon. In 2013, an awarded bursary let her spend a month in Northern India, an experience that birthed a new knowledge of female lives. She's been a staunch feminist ever since. A lover of books and music, Kathryn lives in Falkirk with her border collie, Poppy.

**Rachel Rooney** is a specialist teacher and award-winning children's poet. She has had a number of rhyming picture books and four poetry collections published, including *Hey, Girl!* - her latest book of poems for young teen girls.

**Julie Sheridan** Raised in Ayr, Julie was fascinated by Spanish as a child and spent her pocket money on pocket dictionaries. Her poems have been published in journals including *Lines Review*, *Poetry Scotland*, *Poetry Ireland Review*, *Causeway/Cabhsair* and *PENning*, with upcoming work to feature in *Dreich*. She's lived in Barcelona since 2011.

**Arwen Webb** lives in the Yorkshire Dales, is an NHS trained Aromatherapist and has a Masters in Criminology. She co-founded Richmondshire Writers in 2013. Her poems have appeared in various anthologies and magazines and she performs at local literary events.. She is passionate about women's sex based rights and what it means to be female in a post-modernist world.

**Ali Whitelock** is a Scottish poet living in Australia. *a brief letter to the sea about a couple of things* is her fourth book. Her previous collections include *and my heart crumples like a coke can* and *the lactic acid in the calves of your despair* (long-listed for the Australian Literature Society Gold Medal in 2021). The poem *'do not speak to me of pain'* was a 2020 Pushcart Prize nominee. Her memoir, *poking seaweed with a stick & running away from the smell* was published to critical acclaim in Australia & the UK. www.aliwhitelock.com

**Victoria Whitworth** writes novels, memoirs and other non-fiction. Her 2017 book about Orkney, *Swimming with Seals*, was shortlisted for the Pen Ackerley prize. She has another memoir, *Dust and Pomegranates*, coming out in 2024, as well as a study of the Book of Kells, both with Head of Zeus. Victoria lives in Edinburgh.

# About the Editor

**Magi Gibson** is a poet living and working in Scotland. She has had six poetry collections published. Her signature third collection, *Wild Women of a Certain Age*, first published in 2000, was re-released in an expanded twenty-first anniversary edition in 2021. Her poetry pamphlet '*sixteen poems*', was published in 2022 as her contribution to the global campaign, Sixteen Days of Activism to End Violence Against Women and Girls, with a follow up exhibition as poster poems at the Filia feminist conference in Glasgow in 2023.

Her poetry appears in many anthologies, including *Modern Scottish Women Poets*, *Scottish Love Poems* (both Canongate) and *The Twentieth Century Book of Scottish Poetry* (Edinburgh University Press). As well as in *The Herald*, *The Scotsman*, *The Moth*, *The Stinging Fly*, *Salzburg Literary Review*, *Southbank Review*, *Glasgow Review of Books*, *Northwords Now*, *Cordite* and countless other magazines. Her poems have been broadcast on BBC Radio 4 and BBC Radio Scotland as well as on Melvyn Bragg's ITV series, *Travels in Written Britain*.

She won the Scotland on Sunday/Women 2000 Poetry Prize, the Stirling Open Poetry Competition, was shortlisted for The Asham Short Story Prize and the MacLellan Poetry Prize, and came second in The Scottish International Open Poetry Competition. Her work has been translated into Gaelic, French, German, Norwegian and Japanese.

She founded and edited the poetry magazine, *Pushing Out The Boat*, and was co-editor of *The Poets' Republic* magazine where she was the sole female editor. Through organising and curating multiple regualr Live Literature events from GROWWL in Stirling in the 90s to the ground-breaking DiScOmBoB-uLaTe in Glasgow at both the CCA and the Arches from 2008 – 2011, and more recently the cabaret evening Word Jazzology, she has encouraged and nurtured many younger writers and poets on the Scottish scene.

In 2001 she founded Wild Women Writing and led workshops in Scotland and Ireland in multiple locations including the West Cork Literary Festival and Listowel Writers' Week until she suffered several spine fractures in 2017. Her Wild Women Writing work, along with her work running workshops in women's prisons and for women's refuges and Women's Aid, has given her deep insights into the lives of women.

She has been Writer in Residence in Glasgow's Gållery of Modern Art working with under-privileged youth on the highly praised REBELLAND exhibition, as well as working with inmates of HMP Barlinnie in Glasgow for the GoMA Rule of Thumb exhibition on domestic violence. She was one of the writers in the Barnardo's//Women's Library (London) project 'Prostitution - where now?' working with teens at risk of grooming and prostitution.

She was Scottish Book Trust Reader in Residence in Glasgow Women's Library (2012 - 2015). She's held three Scottish Arts Council Creative Writing Fellowships, is a past Royal Literary Fund Writing Fellow with the University of Paisley, and Creative Scotland awarded her a major bursary for her children's writing. *Seriously Sassy*, her children's novel for 10 to 14 year olds dealing with climate change as well as the ups and downs of being a young teen girl was a finalist in the Green Book Festival Awards in the USA and the Lennoxlove Book Festival Green Book Prize.

In 2023 she was voted by readers of The Scotsman as the third greatest poet from Scotland outside of Robert Burns.

Magi's poetry collections include *Wild Women of a Certain Age*, *Washing Hugh MacDiarmid's Socks*, *I Like Your Hat*, *Graffiti in Red Lipstick*, *Strange Fish*, and *Kicking Back*. Her most recent collections are published by Luath Publishing.

# NOTES ON THE POEMS

### Cíoch/Breast: *Réaltán Ní Leannáin*
*Ann Lovett* was a 15-year-old schoolgirl from Granard, County Longford, Ireland, when she gave birth alone, in the rain, beside a grotto on 31st January 1984. When she was eventually found by some children on their way home from school, her newborn infant son was already dead. Despite an ambulance being called Ann too died shortly after from massive blood loss. Mystery still surrounds many aspects of Ann's pregnancy and death.

### She Remembers Her Husband As Proteus: *Abigail Ottley*
*Proteus*: A sea god from Greek mythology capable of changing form multiple times.

### Shela na gig: *Magi Gibson*
*Sheela na gigs* are ancient figurative carvings of naked women unashamedly displaying their vulvas. They were carved long ago into the stone of churches in Ireland. Pagan in nature, many were eventually destroyed as being too lewd for public display.

*Baubo* in Greek mythology is a small fat older woman - and the goddess of mirth. She is depicted as bawdy and sexually liberated, and is said to have cheered Demeter up when Demeter was mourning the loss of her daughter, Persephone who'd been abducted to the Underworld where forced into marriage. Demeter's spirits were lifted when Baubo made her laugh by lifting her skirt and 'flashing her'. After some time with Baubo, Demeter resolved to continue her quest to save her daughter.

### Manko Taboo: *Jean O'Brien*
*Rukudenashiko* or Megumi Igarashi (Good For Nothing Girl) is a Japanese artist who has been jailed for so-called acts of obscenity by taking casts of her Vulva (Manko).

### The teacher's lovely long red nails: *Katherine Duffy*

*The Children of Lir* is an Irish legend where King Lir's wife dies and his new wife, who no doubt had no choice in marrying the king, becomes jealous of his love for his children. One day, she set out in her chariot with the four children, intending to kill them, but when she ordered her entourage to do the deed, promising them rich rewards, they refused. She drew a sword, but was unable to follow through with the act. She then took the children to Loch Dairbhreach and told them to bathe. Once in the water she cast a spell turning them into swans for three hundred years.

### For Mary: *Lorna Irvine*

*Mary Gordon*, an Edinburgh-based artist and women's rights campaigner, hit the news headlines early in 2021 when she wrote in chalk on the wall of St Andrew's House in Edinburgh, the HQ of the Scottish government as a prtest against the planned Hate Bill. She scribbled "Women's rights are not a hate crime" and "#Women are watching". Afterwards two uniformed police officers interviewed her at her home and advised that any future protests could result in a charge of breach of the peace. "I did it because I feel women's rights are being eroded as is our ability to talk freely and openly about issues which affect us, without being accused of being hateful or transphobic," she later explained. "To write those words in front of the building where these policies are being developed, which are having this chilling impact on women... it felt it was the right thing to do." Mary died in March 2023.

### Bridget Cleary's last message to her friend in the film production company: *Estelle Birdy*

*Bridget Cleary* was just twenty-six in 1895 when she was murdered by her husband at their cottage in Ballyvadlea of County Tipperary, Ireland. He claimed the woman he murdered and immolated was a fairy changeling, not the woman he'd married, and that he had to kill her when repeated and brutal attempts to exorcise her of evil spirits had failed.